HOUSE PLANTS

HOUSE PLANTS

A QUANTUM BOOK

Published by Grange Books
an imprint of Grange Books Plc
The Grange
Kingsnorth Industrial Estate
Hoo, nr. Rochester
Kent ME3 9ND

Copyright ©1998 Quantum Books Ltd

All rights reserved.
This book is protected by copyright. No part of it may be reproduced, stored in a retrieval system, or transmitted in any form or by any means, without the prior permission in writing of the Publisher, nor be otherwise circulated in any form of binding or cover other than that in which it is published and without a similar condition including this condition being imposed on the subsequent publisher.

ISBN 1-84013-141-3

This book is produced by
Quantum Books Ltd
6 Blundell Street
London N7 9BH

Project Manager: Rebecca Kingsley
Project Editor: Judith Millidge
Design/Editorial: David Manson
Andy McColm, Maggie Manson

The material in this publication previously appeared in
Houseplants, Hardy Houseplants,
Houseplant Survival Manual

QUMSPHP
Set in Futura
Reproduced in Singapore by Eray Scan
Printed in Singapore by Star Standard Industries (Pte) Ltd

Contents

HEALTHY HOUSE PLANTS

Almost all the more exciting house plants that we know today originated in the tropics. During the 19th century, there was a passion among botanists for plant-hunting in remote parts of the world. Today, we need look no further than the local garden centre for species which, just a hundred years ago, were to be found only in the depths of the tropical rain forest.

Appreciating House Plants

What can surpass the charms of a house plant gracing a windowsill or cascading from a hanging basket? In appreciating such beauty, it is easy to become a plant collector without realising it.

A TOUCH OF VITALITY

The range of plants offered in flower shops and garden centres has becoming bewilderingly vast. There are plants of every size and shape conceivable, to suit every part of the home. These plants are not merely good to look at, they are *alive* and bring a special touch of brightness and vitality to the home that no china vase or glass ornament ever could. A breath of the vibrant outdoors, whether the home is a country cottage close to the fields and open land or a city apartment hemmed in by steel, asphalt, concrete and city traffic jams.

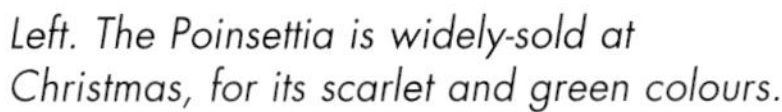

Left. The Poinsettia is widely-sold at Christmas, for its scarlet and green colours.

Above. Rat's Tail Cactus, an exotic, but easy-to-manage plant from Mexico.

A FASCINATING OBSESSION

In fact, plants minister to people's longing for the open countryside. They are forever changing — growing, flowering, resting, ageing, dying. They never allow our interest in them to flag; and they rely upon us for their every need, however modest these may be. In looking after them, we build an active relationship with them. Here then, is the making of a fascinating hobby — which can easily become an obsession.

LIFE-STYLE PLANTS

But what if you are busy? Does such as life-style spell potential disaster for your house plants? Will you have to forgo altogether the great pleasures and company of house plants? Not necessarily. By carefully selecting the most resilient, good-tempered kinds of plant with minimum demands and quick recovery abilities, it is quite possible to enjoy all the benefits of house plants without providing constant care and attention.

Buying House Plants

The tropical heritage of the modern-day house plant has an important bearing, not only on what to buy, but where to buy. When setting out to grow house plants, it is of the utmost importance that the plant should be in good condition to start with.

WHERE TO BUY

In order for a plant to be in good condition, the premises of the plant supplier should be something more than an inadequately-heated and poorly-lit shed. It is important to find a shop that seems warm, well-lit and congenial. The obvious place to start is the established professional plant supplier, but in recent years department stores, supermarkets and garden centres have become an important source of plants for the amateur. Surprising though it may seem, purchases through these stores are often of superior quality to those bought in an ordinary plant shop. As large scale purchasers, stores are able to demand higher quality standards from suppliers, which can be seen in the plant quality.

HEALTH CHECK FOR HOUSE PLANTS

- **CHECK** for firm healthy buds that look capable of flowering. If the plant has been left in a cold draught, the flower buds may drop as soon as the plant is moved.
- **CHECK** for clear unspoilt flowers. Vigorous plants need regular feeding and watering for healthy profuse flowers. Any browning or wilting points to plant starvation.
- **CHECK** for strong well-coloured foliage, free from obvious blemishes. Blister-like spots and brown areas suggest fungus and/or bacterial infection. Rings and mottling may be caused by viruses.
- **CHECK** for clean sturdy stems. A white powdery coating may be mildew, caused by keeping plants in moist stagnant surroundings.

Above. Flaming Katy, Kalanchoe blossfeldiana, a decorative, succulent plant grown for its brightly-coloured, long-lasting flowers.

HEALTH CHECK

You should give your retailer an idea of the conditions which the plant will meet in its new home. A good retailer will enquire about the light and the temperature in your home and will then suggest plants that are likely to do well. Buying a really healthy plant is the key to ensuring indoor gardening success, and to save you disappointment later on, always take time to check the points made in the Health Check table on the facing page.

HOMEWARD-BOUND

Last, but not least, a good plant supplier will carefully wrap the plant for the homeward journey. On a bitterly cold winter's day, you will sometimes see a newly-purchased plant, its leaves blowing in the wind clutched proudly by its new owner who is muffled to the eyes in protective clothing. Even a brief exposure to cold can irreparably damage a plant. If it is cold enough for an overcoat, protect the plant well on the way home.

House Plant Environment

Almost every plant that is brought into the house will present some challenge to the plant grower. In the first place, no matter how good the environment, it is not the stable greenhouse conditions in which the plant has spent the early part of its life.

LIVING PLANTS

Plants are often used as if they are ornaments about the house. Never be tempted to make this mistake as it is a recipe for disaster. It is vital to remember that every plant is a living thing; it has needs that must be satisfied if it is to survive. In the artificial environment of your home, it relies entirely upon you to supply those needs.

LIGHT

Light provides plants with their energy. All plants contain green chlorophyll which traps the energy from sunlight. By the process known as photosynthesis, the chlorophyll then utilises the light to manufacture sugars and other complex chemicals by absorbing carbon dioxide from the air and hydrogen and oxygen from water.

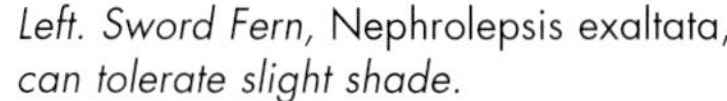

Left. Sword Fern, Nephrolepsis exaltata, *can tolerate slight shade.*

Above. Primula obconica, *a colourful, resilient, house plant.*

AIR AND VENTILATION

Most of us like to get some fresh air into our homes and house plants appreciate fresh air too. Whereas humans inhale oxygen and exhale carbon dioxide, plant metabolism operates in reverse, absorbing carbon dioxide and expelling oxygen. Humans and plants both welcome the effect of ventilation, provided that it is warm enough. Always ventilate with some thought to the outdoor conditions and never to excess. Be ready to provide more water to compensate for the moisture removed by air currents.

TEMPERATURE

As so many foliage plants come from the tropical forests and because most cacti are desert plants, you might well think that the hotter you keep the house, the more the house plants will like it. But this is not so. Provided that you can ensure temperatures of 7–24°C (45–75°F) — a range that most people maintain for their own comfort anyway — then you need have few worries about your plants. It is also important to avoid wildly fluctuating high and low temperatures, as few plants can cope with these easily.

Watering and Feeding

'How much water should I give my plants?' is the most frequent of all questions about house plants. Give the plant too little and their leaves droop, too much and their foliage yellows. Is it possible to strike a balance?

WATERING

If plants are dry pour water onto the surface of the soil. Pour until you can see the surplus draining through the bottom of the pot. If the plant is very dry, then it should be submerged in a bucket of water. Hold the pot with your fingers and place your thumbs on the soil before plunging it in. Leave the pot in the water until all the air bubbles have escaped. If the plant is still thirsty, this exercise can be repeated at every watering (twice or three times a week). Rainwater is generally better for plants that object to lime, but it is not essential. It is important not to use very cold water, direct from the tap when watering some plants, such as African Violets. The best practice is to fill a watering can and leave it to stand in a heated room or on a radiator overnight.

Left. Watering is a matter of care with the African Violet, Saintpaulia ionantha.

Above. Feeding is not required by Chrysanthemum morifolium.

FEEDING

Your plant will have come from a nursery where it was fed regularly. This practice must continue when the plant is taken home, or it will suffer loss of colour and general decline in health. An extensive range of fertilisers, in various forms is available from most garden centres and the one most suitable for your plants is very often a question of trial and error. Probably, fertiliser in liquid form is the best, as it can be more easily absorbed by plants, but two other different types of fertiliser are outlined in the table on the right.

FERTILISERS FOR HOUSE PLANTS

- **PELLET FEEDS** are pushed into the soil. When the plant is watered, the pellet releases the correct dosage of feed,

- **FERTILISER STICKS** are pushed into the soil at the edge of the pot. They release nutrients over a given period of time.

- **LIQUID FEEDS** can be given to the plant when it is watered. Powdered feed can be diluted in water to form a liquid feed.

HOUSE PLANT SPECIES

Key to symbols

The following icons are used throughout the directory to help provide a snapshot of the care that each species requires.

Light. Amount required with 4 the greatest and 0 the least.

Watering. Amount required with 4 the greatest and 0 the least.

Feeding. Amount required with 4 the greatest and 0 the least.

Total care. Amount of care required expressed as a total of the other three items above with 12 the greatest and 0 the least.

THROUGHOUT THE DIRECTORY
The botanical name for the species is given first in alphabetical order, followed by the common name.

AECHMEA FASCIATA URN PLANT

One of the largest bromeliads, forming a rosette of tough, spiny-edged, grey-green leaves, irregularly cross-banded with silver. When mature it produces a flower from its centre, bearing a cluster of pink bracts, from which flowers briefly appear.

Family Bromeliaceae.
Light Good sunlight.
Temperature 15–24°C (60–75°F).
Care Weak liquid feed every two weeks from spring to autumn.
Watering Maintain a reservoir at the centre of the leaves, with soft water.

AEONIUM ARBOREUM TREE AEONIUM

This is a taller, branching species, unlike most aeoiums which are ground-hugging. Each branch carries a typical aeonium rosette at the end. It is an eye-catching plant. It has a purple leaved form 'Atropurpureum' which is quite distinctive.

Family Crassulaceae.
Light Good light and sun.
Temperature 15–24°C (60–75°F).
Care Liquid feed fortnightly in growing season.
Watering Moderate while growing, only enough to prevent parching.

AGAVE AMERICANA CENTURY PLANT

Named because it is said only to flower once in a hundred years. It does take many years to flower and the rosette of leaves dies when the flowers fade. Grown in the home for its spiny-edged blue-green leaves. A less vigorous form known as 'Marginata' has creamy margins to its leaves.

Family Agavaceae.
Light Good but not strong.
Temperature 15–24°C (60–75°F).
Care Liquid feed fortnightly while actively growing.
Watering Moderate in summer, minimum in winter to keep just moist.

AGLAONEMA CRISPUM SILVER QUEEN

One of several aglaonemas grown for their ornamental variegated leaves. As members of the arum family, they do form typical flowers in summer, but these are small, greenish-yellow and insignificant.

Family Araceae.
Light Good but not strong.
Temperature 18–21°C (65–70°F).
Care Liquid feed once a month, except in mid-winter.
Watering Moderate while actively growing; very little while resting. Always keep moist.

ANANAS COMOSUS VARIEGATUS ORNAMENTAL PINEAPPLE

This is a strikingly decorative form of the cultivated pineapple, of which we enjoy the fruits. It is a terrestrial rather than tree-dwelling bromeliad and has arching spiny-edged leaves, with broad, ivory margins.

Family Bromeliaceae.
Light Bright light is essential.
Temperature 18–24°C (65–75°F).
Care Liquid feed twice a month throughout the year as this plant has no resting period.
Watering Moderate throughout the year, letting it partly dry out between waterings.

ANTHURIUM SCHERZERIANUM FLAMINGO FLOWER

This is a member of the arum family. It makes a compact plant with dark, glossy-green, spear-shaped leaves from among which rise its flowering stems, each bearing a brilliant scarlet spathe.

Family Araceae.
Light Moderate as it is adapted to jungle.
Temperature 18–24°C (65–75°F).
Care Liquid feed fortnightly while actively growing.
Watering Generous while growing; restrained during mid-winter, but maintain high humidity.

APHELANDRA SQUARROSA LOUISAE ZEBRA PLANT

This plant take its common name from thc prominent ivory-white veins on it glossy dark-green leaves. This tropical foliage plant forms a tall flowers spike in spring, with yellow bracts bearing short-lived yellow flowers.

Family Acanthaceae.
Light Good but not fierce light.
Temperature 18–24°C (65–75°F).
Care Feed this hungry plant every week, while growing, and not when resting.
Watering Keep compost moist while growing and barely moist when at rest.

APOROCACTUS FLAGELLIFORMIS RAT'S TAIL CACTUS

The pendulous growth makes this plant ideally suited to a hanging basket, a pot suspended on wires, or on a shelf so the stems can hang freely. It is a spectacular sight with stems overflowing with dozens of long crimson-red flowers.

Family Cactaceae.
Light Good filtered light.
Temperature 18–24°C (65–75°F).
Care A high-potash feed every fortnight while actively growing.
Watering Generous amounts to keep compost moist while actively growing. Keep just moist in winter.

ARAUCARIA HETEROPHYLLA NORFOLK ISLAND PINE

This is by nature a tall-growing conifer from Norfolk Island (Australia) that can reach 60m (200ft) high, and is a relative of the monkey puzzle tree. When young, it can make a Christmas-tree-like foliage plant.

Family Araucariaceae.
Light Good light, will shed its needles in shade.
Temperature 7–24°C (45–75°F).
Care Liquid feed twice a month from spring to autumn.
Watering Plenty while growing, only just moist in winter.

ASPARAGUS DENSIFLORUS ASPARAGUS FERN

This is one of the most resilient of the so-called Asparagus Ferns, grown indoors for their feathery foliage. They are members of the lily family and cousins of the vegetable asparagus. They form long trailing stems and are at their best in a hanging basket.

Family Liliaceae.
Light Good light, not fierce sun.
Temperature 15–24°C (60–75°F).
Care Liquid feed fortnightly while growing.
Watering Generous in summer to keep really moist. Only enough to keep just moist in winter.

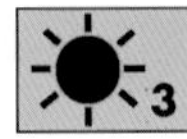

ASPIDISTRA ELATIOR CAST IRON PLANT

Named after its cast iron constitution. They make handsome plants with their shapely foliage and glossy-green leaves. Flowers form at soil level and are dull purple. 'Variegata' is a form with creamy white stripes along its leaves.

Family Liliaceae.
Light Moderately good light. 'Variegata' needs good light.
Temperature 7–27°C (45–80°F).
Care Liquid feed fortnightly while growing.
Watering Moderate through the year, partly drying out between waterings. Overwatering harms the leaves.

ASPLENIUM NIDUS BIRD'S NEST FERN

A tropical fern growing on trees in the South Pacific and Australia. It has undivided fronds, more like the leaves of flowering plants, forming a bowl-shaped plant, hence the name bird's nest fern.

Family Polypodiaceae.
Light Moderate suits it best.
Temperature 15°C (60°F) minimum.
Care Liquid feed fortnightly when actively growing.
Watering Really moist while growing. Barely moist in winter. Plunge pot in damp peat or stand on damp pebbles to create humid air around the plant.

BEGONIA CORALLINA 'LUCERNA' SPOTTED ANGEL WING BEGON

A highly decorative plant both for its foliage and clusters of coral-pink flowers. It is very easy to strike plantlets from stem cuttings. The elephant's-ear-shaped leaves are bright green with white spots above and wine-red spots underneath.

Family Begoniaceae.
Light Good light essential to get full colouring. Strong light scorches leaves.
Temperature 18–24° (65–75°F).
Care Liquid feed twice a month.
Watering Moderate in the growing season. The top compost should never be allowed to dry out between waterings. In winter keep barely moist.

BEGONIA REX REX BEGONIA

Begonia Rex is the group name for hybrids grown for their exceptionally beautifully coloured and marked leaves. They may flower, but the blossoms are insignificant. Leaf colouring varies from silvery green to almost black-purple. Happiest in shallow pots, they are deciduous, the leaves dying in poor winter light.

Family Begoniaceae.
Light Good but not strong light.
Temperature 18–24° (65–75°F).
Care Liquid feed twice a month.
Watering Moderate during growing season. Keep barely moist in winter.

BELOPERONE GUTTATA SHRIMP PLANT

This plant does produce very authentic-looking shrimps. The 'shrimps' are formed from overlapping pinkish brown bracts, from which tiny white flowers briefly appear. It has a straggly nature so must be kept in shape and size.

Family Acanthaceae.
Light Good light with some sun.
Temperature 18–24° (65–75°F).
Care Liquid feed twice a month while growing.
Watering Just enough to keep compost moist but allow the top surface to dry out between waterings.

BILLBERGIA NUTANS QUEEN'S TEARS/ FRIENDSHIP PLANT

This is a tough, easily-managed, terrestrial bromeliad from Brazil and Argentina. It forms long flowering stems clothed in long pink bracts. From these hang nodding clusters of dainty flowers. Its arching grey-green leaves are tubular at the base and form clustered rosettes of growth.

Family Bromeliaceae.
Light Good light and some direct sunlight needed to produce flowers.
Temperature 7–24°C (45–75°F).
Care Liquid feed twice a month.
Watering Keep compost moist all the time as there is no rest period.

CAMPANULA ISOPHYLLA ITALIAN BELLFLOWER

A traditional favourite for a country cottage windowsill. Today, it is often displayed as a trailing plant, or in a hanging basket. The flowers are either china-blue or white depending on the variety. The flowers, if well looked after, will bloom until the autumn. An easy-to-please plant.

Family Campanulaceae.
Light Good light with no fierce sun.
Temperature 15–24°C (60–75°F).
Care Liquid feed twice a month.
Watering Enough to keep the compost moist in summer; less in winter.

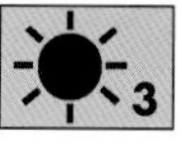

CEROPEGIA WOODII ROSARY VINE/HEARTS ON A STRING

A plant that is both succulent and a trailer suitable for a hanging basket. Its stringy stems carry many scattered heart-shaped fleshy leaves, like beads on a rosary. The flowers are small, tubular and purple.

Family Asclepiadaceae.
Light Good light with several hours of sun each day.
Temperature 15–24°C (60–75°F).
Care Liquid feed monthly while growing strongly.
Watering Moderate in active growing season, minimum in winter.

CHAMAECEREUS SILVESTRII PEANUT CACTUS

This cactus, so called from the appearance of its young stems, is a typical, easily-managed small desert cactus for the home. Although small, it is quite a strong grower, quickly filling a pot with side growths, which can be detached to form a ready means of propagation.

Family Cactaceae.
Light Plenty of light.
Temperature 15–24°C (60—75°F).
Care Liquid feed every 3–5 weeks during growing season
Watering Moderately when actively growing. Barely moist during winter.

CHAMAEDOREA ELEGANS PARLOUR PALM

Often sold under the name *Neanthe bella*, it is useful in the home as it is shorter than most palms. It takes several years to reach 90cm (3ft). An easy plant to manage, provided it gets enough moisture and not too much heat or light.

Family Palmae.
Light Good, filtered light.
Temperature 18–24°C (65–75°F).
Care Weak liquid feed monthly in growing season.
Watering Plenty during growing season, keeping compost moist. Reduce in winter, so that compost is just moist.

CHRYSANTHEMUM MORIFOLIUM POT CHRYSANTHEMUM

Among the most popular of all indoor flowering plants. Their period of beauty lasts from six to eight weeks and after that it is not possible to keep the plants. They are available every month of the year and so are easy to replace. Their main requirements are good light, moderate warmth and enough water. Their blooms may be white, yellow, bronze, pink or orange.

Family Compositae.
Light Good light, but no fierce sun.
Temperature 10–18°C (50–65°F).
Care No feeding as temporary plants.
Watering Keep compost moist.

CISSUS ANTARTICA KANGAROO VINE

A vigorous, handsome, climbing plant that clings by its tendrils as it goes. A relative of the grape vine, it is valued for its shiny, evergreen, oval, pointed leaves and tolerance of a wide range of room conditions.

Family Vitaceae.
Light Bright sunlight; tolerates shade.
Temperature 18–21°C (65–70°F).
Care Liquid feed twice a month from spring to autumn.
Watering Moderate while growing and when the surface of the compost shows a need. Minimum during winter.

CLIVIA MINIATA KAFFIR LILY

The orange-flowered Kaffir Lily from South Africa, is a valuable flowering houseplant that should bring pleasure for a number of years with minimum care. Its main demands are adequate light and a winter rest period.

Family Amaryllidaceae.
Light Bright light with some sun.
Temperature 15–24°C (60–75°F).
Care Liquid feed twice a month once flower stems are half grown.
Watering Plenty to keep moist and fleshy roots plump, during growing season. Minimum in winter.

COLEUS BLUMEI FLAME NETTLE/PAINTED NETTLE

A tropical plant grown for its highly coloured, patterned leaves. It does produce spikes of pale blue flowers but these are best removed. Vigorous plants that demand plenty of food, water and light while growing.

Family Labiatae.
Light Bright light, with some direct sun, to ensure colouring and growth.
Temperature 15–24°C (60–75°F).
Care Liquid feed twice a month.
Watering As often as necessary to keep compost really moist. They quickly wilt if water is withheld. Mist foliage daily to deter red spider mites.

CRASSULA FALCATA THE PROPELLER PLANT

Named after the shape of its grey-blue leaves, which are somewhat twisted. This is a sprawling, bushy plant by nature, but the young plant for a time forms just a single upright stem. Its bright scarlet flowers are quite showy and contrast with the blue of the leaves.

Family Crassulaceae.
Light Good light and plenty of sun.
Temperature 15–24°C (60–75°F).
Care Liquid feed fortnightly while growing.
Watering Moderate in summer, little in winter to keep barely damp.

CRYPTANTHUS BIVITTATUS EARTH STAR

One of the smallest of the bromeliads grown ornamentally. It is a terrestrial species growing in crevices and fallen trees and uses its root system to anchor it, rather than for absorbing food.

Family Bromeliaceae.
Light Good light all year round to produce good leaf colour.
Temperature 15–24°C (60–75°F).
Care Feeding unnecessary but occasionally foliar-feed while in active growth.
Watering Only enough to keep the compost just moist.

DIEFFENBACHIA MACULATA DUMB CANE

A highly decorative foliage plant which tolerates cooler temperatures and lower humidity than most dieffenbachias. It has poisonous sap, which can cause serious mouth and throat problems, so always wash your hands after taking cuttings from this plant.

Family Araceae.
Light Moderate in summer, good light in winter.
Temperature 18–27°C (65–80°F).
Care Liquid feed fortnightly.
Watering Moderate to keep compost moist. Barely moist in winter.

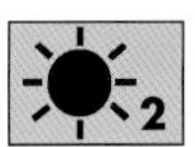

DRACAENA MARGINATA MADAGASCAR DRAGON TREE

D. Marginata 'Tricolour' is a neat and attractive form of Dragon Tree with many graceful arching leaves growing from the cane-like stem. It has a cream band between the narrow red border and the green leaf colour. This plant can grow to 2.4m (8ft).

Family Agavaceae.
Light Good light but not full sun.
Temperature 18–24°C (65–75°F).
Care Liquid feed fortnightly while actively growing.
Watering Generous to keep compost moist. Little in winter rest period.

ECHEVERIA ELEGANS MEXICAN GEM

A neat, rosette-shaped succulent plant that has fleshy blue-grey leaves covered with a white bloom. Sometimes planted in floral clocks but useful as a windowsill plant. It produces clusters of tubular pink and yellow flowers carried on high stems in summer.

Family Crassulaceae.
Light Full light, even strong sun.
Temperature 15–24°C (60–75°F).
Care Weak feed twice a month.
Watering Water with restraint even in growing season. Give only enough to prevent shrivelling. Keep water off the leaves as they will rot or scorch.

ECHINOCACTUS GRUSONII GOLDEN BARREL CACTUS

Sometimes referred to as Mother-in-Law's Cushion, this is a slow-growing plant. It is unlikely to flower in the home because it needs to grow large before doing so. Its main attractions are its symmetrical form—many tubercles aligned as vertical ribs and many golden spines.

Family Cactaceae.
Light Plenty of light.
Temperature 15–24°C (60–75°F).
Care Liquid feed every 3-5 weeks during growing season.
Watering Moderately when actively growing. Barely moist during winter.

ECHINOCEREUS PECTINATUS HEDGEHOG CACTUS

This is a neat grower ideally suited for growth on a bright windowsill in a warm room. It takes about six years to reach 10cm (4in) in height, after which its single-ribbed stem may branch. It bears clusters of white spines at the areoles on these ribs. Its typical cactus flowers are mauve-pink.

Family Cactaceae.
Light Plenty of light.
Temperature 15–24°C (60–75°F).
Care Liquid feed every 3-5 weeks when actively growing.
Watering Moderately during growing period. Barely moist in winter.

EPIPHYLLUM 'ACKERMANNII' ORCHID CACTUS

Also known as *Nopalxochia ackermannii,* this garden hybrid is a magnificent plant when in flower in spring. It boasts huge flowers which, although by no means orchid-shaped, are as splendid as those of a real orchid.

Family Cactaceae.
Light Moderate light.
Temperature 15–27°C (60–80°F).
Care High-potash feed every fortnight.
Watering Plenty in summer, moderate at all other times, except a minimum of water for a three-week rest period after flowering.

EUPHORBIA MILLI CROWN OF THORNS

A drought-resistant member of this large genus of plants, which originate from Madagascar. It is grown for its rather bizarre beauty, its thorny shrubby growth, somewhat sparse foliage and tiny bright scarlet 'flowers' (really bracts) like drops of blood.

Family Euphorbiaceae.
Light All the light and sun you can give it.
Temperature 15–27°C (60–80°F).
Care Liquid feed fortnightly during season of active growth.
Watering Enough to keep compost moist in summer. Minimum in winter.

EUPHORBIA PULCHERRIMA POINSETTIA

Far better known as the Poinsettia, and now widely sold as a Christmas pot plant. Its bright scarlet bracts are its main attraction, and remain colourful for about a couple of months. They are not flowers but coloured leaves.

Family Euphorbiaceae.
Light Good light but not fierce sun.
Temperature 15–21°C (60–70°F).
Care Bought plants need no feeding while in 'flower'. If plants are retained, liquid feed monthly while growing.
Watering Moderate to keep compost just moist.

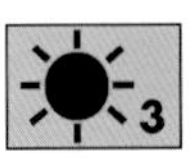

FATSHEDERA LIZEI TREE IVY

An evergreen foliage plant which is a hybrid between, *Fatsia japonica* and the Irish ivy, *Hedera helix hibernica*. There is also a distinctive variegated form, marked with white along the leaf margins. This is an easily managed, tough plant.

Family Araliaceae.
Light Moderate light, 'Variegata' needs stronger light.
Temperature 15–24°C (60–75°F).
Care Liquid feed twice a month.
Watering Moderate, reduce in midwinter when at rest. Keep moist at the roots or leaves could fall.

FATSIA JAPONICA 'VARIEGATA' CASTOR OIL PLANT

Also known as the Figleaf Palm, this is an exotic-looking foliage plant with large leaves shaped like hands with seven to nine finger-like lobes. It is a hardy shrub, happy in the garden, bearing clusters of white flowers in late winter. Pruning may be needed to keep the plant within bounds.

Family Araliaceae.
Light Good light, tolerate some shade.
Temperature 10–21°C (50–70°F).
Care Liquid feed fortnightly.
Watering Generous in growing season, enough in winter to prevent the compost completely drying out.

FAUCARIA TIGRINA TIGER JAWS

A South African succulent which mimics a tiger's jaws in the shape of its long fleshy leaves, and the hooked teeth with which they are armed. Its yellow flowers look not unlike daisies, add to the tiger picture by their colour. This plant grows by means of basal offsets and is grown for its interesting shape.

Family Aizoaceae.
Light Good light and some sun.
Temperature 15–24°C (60–75°F).
Care Weak feed monthly when growing.
Watering Enough to keep compost moist; in winter very little needed.

FICUS BENJAMINA WEEPING FIG

A graceful plant which is by nature a tree and will continue to grow taller and may become too large for a house. An undemanding plant able to cope with a large range of conditions. Scale insects may appear so keep the foliage clean.

Family Moraceae.
Light Moderate with e few hours of sun a day. Variegated from needs more light to keep its colour.
Temperature 15–24°C (60–75°F).
Care Liquid feed twice a month.
Watering Moderate, allow surface to dry out between each watering.

FICUS ELASTICA RUBBER PLANT

A popular evergreen foliage plant for home decoration. Its glossy leaves are a magnificent rich dark green. Usually grown as a single-stemmed specimen, this fiscus can branch to form a bushier specimen. Easy to care for but correct watering is essential to stop leaf drop. Sponge the leaves regularly to remove dust and grime.

Family Moraceae.
Light Moderate with some sun.
Temperature 15–24°C (60–75°F).
Care Liquid feed twice a month.
Watering Moderate to keep just moist. Dislikes too much water.

FICUS PUMILA CREEPING FIG

A creeping foliage plant from East Asia valuable for furnishing and spreading over a support. It forms small heart-shaped leaves on thin wiry stems. The form 'Variegata' has white edges and is less vigorous.

Family Moraceae.
Light Moderate with some sun; variegated form needs more light to keep its colour.
Temperature 15–24°C (60–75°F).
Care Liquid feed twice a month.
Watering Moderate to keep just moist. Surface should be allowed to dry out between waterings.

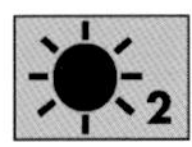

GASTERIA VERRUCOSA WARTY GASTERIA

A succulent grown for its distinctive clumps of fleshy leaves and tall tubular flowers, which appear in late spring and early summer. Its tapering leaves are covered in whitish warts referred to as in its epithet *verrucosa*.

Family Liliaceae.
Light Moderate light, no direct sun.
Temperature 15–24°C (60–75°F).
Care None, because it forces unnatural growth.
Watering Moderate while growing, let it partly dry out between waterings. Keep barely moist in winter.

GREVILLEA ROBUSTA SILK OAK

The Australian Silk Oak makes a forest tree of 30m (100ft) high in a suitable environment. Indoors it makes a ferny-leaved evergreen foliage plant which looks good with plants with contrasting foliage.

Family Proteaceae.
Light Bright light, and as much light as possible in winter.
Temperature 15–24°C (60–75°F).
Care Provide high humidity in summer and liquid feed monthly while growing.
Watering Keep the compost moist. In winter, keep barely moist.

GYMNOCALYCIUM QUELHIANUM ROSE PLAID CACTUS

The Rose Plaid Cactus is a flattened globular shape, growing slowly to 12.5cm (5in) across but only 5cm (2in) high. In summer it opens white flowers tinged with red in the centre. Other species of gymnocalycium have red or yellow flowers.

Family Cactaceae
Light Plenty of light.
Temperature 15–24°C (60–75°F).
Care Liquid feed every 3-5 weeks during growing season.
Watering Moderately when actively growing. Barely moist in winter.

GYNURA SARMENTOSA PURPLE PASSION VINE

This is a trailing plant of the daisy family, treasured for its purple-haired foliage. It is a handsome plant while young but tends to become straggly with age. Prune back its growths to keep compact, and replace with a new plant from a cutting every second year.

Family Compositae.
Light Good light with some sun.
Temperature 15–24°C (60–75°F).
Care Liquid feed fortnightly all year round to help growth.
Watering Moderate in summer. Minimum in winter. Keep water off the leaves or they will mark in bright light.

HAWORTHIA MARGARITIFERA PEARL PLANT

This is a spiky-leaved South African succulent plant often grown on sunny windowsills. It quickly forms offsets around the main rosette. Similar in appearance to the houseleek, this haworthia is distinguished by the warty, white markings on its leaves, from where it gets its name. Tiny tubular flowers form once the plant is mature.

Family Liliceae.
Light Good light, but no direct sun.
Temperature 15–24°C (60–75°F).
Care No feeding required.
Watering Moderate in summer, barely moist in winter.

HEDERA CANARIENSIS 'VARIEGATA' CANARY ISLAND IVY

Although closely related to the common ivy, it has larger leaves and generally softer growth. Once acclimatised to the outdoors, it is reasonably hardy. The leaves are grey-green and cream and stalks red. Often known as 'Gloire de Marengo', this variegated form is suitable for training over canes or trellis.

Family Araliaceae.
Light Good light with some sun.
Temperature Very tolerant, needs extra humidity and high temperatures.
Care Liquid feed twice a month.
Watering Keep compost quite moist.

HEDERA HELIX 'GLACIER' ENGLISH IVY

This ivy has typical ivy leaves which are variegated mid-green and grey-green with white splashes and pink edges. Less vigorous than the original species, the growing tips should be pinched out to keep it bushy.

Family Araliaceae.
Light Good light and some sun.
Temperature Very tolerant but needs humidity. Mist frequently as red spider mite can be a problem.
Care Liquid feed twice a month.
Watering Quite moist while growing, less in winter.

HELIOTROPIUM PERUVIANUM HELIOTROPE

This plant is valued for its purple flowers and for its sweet, rich scent reminiscent of cherry pie. By nature a shrubby plant that becomes woody at the base, it can be kept for some years. As flowering deteriorates with age, it is best to use new plants each year. Treat as a temporary plant. Watch out for pests, particularly whitefly which love it.

Family Boraginaceae.
Light Good light, no fierce sun.
Temperature 15–21°C (60–70°F).
Care Liquid feed fortnightly while growing.
Watering Moderate to keep moist.

HELXINE SOLEIROLII BABY'S TEARS/ MIND YOUR OWN BUSINESS

Recently renamed *Soleirolia soleirolii*, this plant is a creeping specimen related to the stinging nettle. A strong grower, it will spread if not contained. Grown in small pots, it forms pleasing hummocks of fresh green foliage. There is also a gold-leaved form, which looks just like sunshine if it gets enough light.

Family Urticaceae.
Light Good light to moderate shade.
Temperature 10–24°C (50–75°F).
Care Weak liquid feed fortnightly while growing.
Watering Keep moist at all times.

HEPTAPLEURUM ARBORICOLA PARASOL PLANT

An evergreen whose common name derives from the radiating leaflets. Left alone, it will rapidly grow into a tree-like specimen. It lends itself to training and if the growing tip is pinched out, will form a bushy plant more suitable for indoors.

Family Araliaceae.
Light Good light, not full sun.
Temperature 15–24°C (60–75°F).
Care Liquid feed fortnightly when growing.
Watering Moderate. Keep the compost moist.

HIBISCUS ROSA-SINENSIS ROSE OF CHINA

A strong growing sub-tropical shrub, widely used as a decorative garden plant. It forms a brilliant display of large, trumpet flowers. Pruning may be needed in early spring to ensure a compact plant in the spring. The exotic blooms are worth any effort needed to produce them.

Family Malvaceae.
Light Good light but not full sun.
Spread 15–24°C (60–75°F).
Care High-potash feed twice monthly while actively growing.
Watering Keep moist at all times. Spray foliage with water on warm days.

HIPPEASTRUM HYBRID AMARYLLIS

One of the most striking of all bulb flowers, usually bought as dry bulbs, potted, and then flower in late winter or early spring. They have a dormant period when the foliage dies off. The large flowers can be four to a stem. Two stems arise from the largest bulbs.

Family Amaryllidaceae.
Light Good light. Affected by light while dormant.
Temperature 15–18°C (60–65°F).
Care Liquid feed twice a month through to mid-summer, then high-potash feed until spring.
Watering Moderate to keep moist.

HOWEA FORSTERIANA PARADISE PALM /KENTIA

This is a stronger-growing plant than *Chamaedorea* forming a small tree in a few years, with arching stems, bearing many leaflets held out horizontally. Allow plenty of space for this plant when choosing your room decoration.

Family Palmaceae.
Light Good, filtered light.
Temperature 18–24°C (65–75°F).
Care Weak liquid feed monthly when growing.
Watering Plenty when growing and adequate drainage. Less in winter to keep compost moist.

HOYA CARNOSA HONEY PLANT/ WAX PLANT/ PORCELAIN FLOWER

An easily-grown, climbing plant, valued for its clusters of long-lasting sweet-scented flowers, which appear from late spring to early autumn. It can be trained over an indoor trellis or in a large pot, around a ring of wire. This concentrates its flowers for an intense effect.

Family Asclepiadaceae.
Light Good light with a few hours sun.
Temperature 10–21°C (50–70°F).
Care High-potash feed fortnightly while growing.
Watering Moderate to keep moist.

HYPOESTES PHYLLOSTACHYA FRECKLE FACE

Also known as the Polka Dot plant, it is grown solely for its foliage, which is deep olive green with pink freckles. It is cheerful to have on a windowsill where it can enjoy plenty of light. Without good light, its pink colouring fades and may disappear. Insignificant flowers are formed but are best removed.

Family Acanthaceae.
Light Bright but filtered light.
Temperature 15–24°C (60–75°F).
Care Liquid feed fortnightly while growing.
Watering Moderate to keep moist, less in winter when semi-dormant.

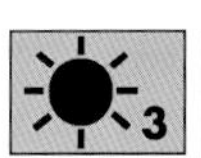

JASMINE POLYANTHUM PINK JASMINE

A strong-growing climber cultivated for its white flowers, flushed with pink on the outside and sweetly scented. It flowers early from late winter to early spring. It does demand good light in which to thrive and is vigorous, and requires pruning after flowering.

Family Oleaceae.
Light Bright light with some sun.
Temperature 7–15°C (45–60°F).
Care Liquid feed twice a month while growing.
Watering Plenty while growing, drier when semi-dormant in winter.

KALANCHOE BLOSSFELDIANA FLAMING KATY

A decorative succulent plant, grown for its brightly-coloured long-lasting flowers which are usually brilliant scarlet, though there are magenta-pink, yellow and orange forms. It will not flower again under home conditions so is best discarded

Family Crassulaceae.
Light Give plenty of light on a sunny windowsill.
Temperature 15–24°C (60–75°F).
Care Liquid feed once or twice a month.
Watering Restrained or the leaves become flabby and flowering reduced.

KALANCHOE DAIGREMONTIANA DEVIL'S BACKBONE

This is a succulent plant and makes a fascinating windowsill plant. Tiny plantlets form on its leaf margins and provide a very ready means of making new plants. This is a single stem variety with fleshy tooth-edged leaves. It may flower but the blooms are tiny and uninteresting.

Family Crassulaceae.
Light Good light.
Temperature 15–24°C (60–75°F).
Care Liquid feed monthly.
Watering Moderate in summer, very sparingly in winter.

LAURUS NOBILIS LAUREL/ BAY TREE

An evergreen bush or small tree often planted as a formal clipped specimen in a patio tub. It can be used indoors as a shapely foliage plant. Naturally forms a spreading bush shape which is easily trimmed to create a more formal shape, usually that of a cone.

Family Lauraceae.
Light Bright light and direct sunlight.
Temperature 7–24°C (45–75°F).
Care Liquid feed monthly when growing.
Watering Moderate from spring to early autumn, it must never dry out. Drier in winter, as cold wet soil can kill it.

LIRIOPE MUSCARI BIG BLUE LILY TURF

A hardy garden plant that was introduced from China and Japan purely for the spikes of purple-blue flowers. It grows with a clusters of strap-like leaves springing from soil level. More decorative is the form 'Variegata' with leaves striped yellow along their length.

Family Liliaceae.
Light Good light.
Temperature 13–21°C (55–70°F).
Care Liquid feed fortnightly.
Watering Moderate to keep compost moist when growing. Just enough in winter to prevent parching.

LITHOPS FULLERI LIVING STONES

One of several species of succulent plants that eke out an existence in the deserts of Southern Africa and mimic pebbles. Their appeal as house plants is limited as they are very small and not very showy. They develop into clumps, but progress is slow.

Family Aizoaceae.
Light Good with some direct sun each day.
Temperature 15–24°C (60–75°F).
Care So sparse is their diet, they need no feeding from us.
Watering Minimum to keep compost moist. During the winter rest period, give none.

MARANTA LEUCONEURA KERCHOVEANA PRAYER PLANT

A favourite foliage house plant, compact, attractive and easy to look after. Its leaves fold together at night, hence its name. This form is also known as Rabbit Tracks with dark brown marking between the veins likened to rabbit tracks. A jungle plant from South America it likes warmth and high humidity.

Family Marantaceae.
Light Moderate to prevent leaf scorch.
Temperature 18–24°C (65–75°F).
Care Liquid feed fortnightly when growing.
Watering Plenty of water as they like tropical conditions.

MONSTERA DELICIOSA SWISS CHEESE PLANT

One of the most widely grown of all foliage house plants; it is tough and long-lived. By nature it is thick-stemmed and climbs, so some support is essential. A moss pole suits it well and the aerial roots can be trained into the moss or into the pot compost.

Family Araceae.
Light Good but filtered light in summer. Best possible light in winter.
Temperature 15–24°C (60–75°F).
Care Liquid feed twice a month.
Watering Keep compost barely moist; allow surface to dry out slightly.

NEOREGELIA CAROLINAE 'TRICOLOUR' BLUSHING BROMELIAD

A highly decorative bromeliad which has a rich, beetroot-red colour in the centre of its leaf rosette, which develops as flowering time approaches. Tiny, insignificant flowers develop in the vase, untroubled by wet conditions. The leaves are marked with yellow stripes which contrast with the reddish heart.

Family Bromeliaceae.
Light Good sunlight.
Temperature 15–24°C (60–75°F).
Care Weak liquid feed every 2 weeks from spring to autumn.
Watering Maintain a reservoir at the centre of the leaves, with soft water.

NEPHROLEPIS EXALTATA SWORD FERN

A vigorous grower producing a cluster of fronds, each divided into many pinnae ('feathers'). It can develop into a most handsome foliage plant, able to tolerate shade. This fern grows from a rhizome from which it sends out wiry runners with plantlets on the ends.

Family Polypodiaceae.
Light Good light, tolerates light shade.
Temperature 15–24°C (60–75°F).
Care Liquid feed monthly, in soil-based compost, and twice monthly in peat-based compost.
Watering Plenty to keep compost moist all the time.

PELARGONIUM GRAVEOLENS GERANIUM

This is one of a number of species grown for their scented foliage. This particular kind is scented of roses, others offer peppermint, lemon or apple scent. *P.graveolens* produces rose-pink flowers with tiny purple spots on them. A vigorous plant, its leaves are deeply segmented and quite ornamental.

Family Geraniaceae.
Light Good light.
Temperature 15–24°C (60–75°F).
Care Liquid feed with high-potash twice a month, while growing.
Watering Moderate while growing.

PEPEROMIA ARGYREIA

Once known as *P. sandersii,* this plant has smooth-surfaced, rather fleshy leaves, marked with alternate green and silver bands which radiate outwards from the leaf stalk. Its name *argyreia* means 'silvery'. It dislikes overwatering but otherwise is an easy plant.

Family Piperaceae.
Light Good light but no intense sun.
Temperature 15–24°C (60–75°F).
Care Weak liquid feed monthly while actively growing.
Watering Provide moderate amounts, letting compost dry out partly between waterings. Keep compost just moist.

PEPEROMIA MAGNOLIFOLIA 'VARIEGATA' DESERT PRIVET

This has typical heart-shaped peperomia foliage is a taller specimen. Its stems tend to flop and become creeping as it reaches maturity. Its form 'Variegata' is a green-and-gold variegated plant, always sunny to look at, provided that it receives enough light to retain its full colouring.

Family Piperaceae.
Light Good sunlight.
Temperature 15–24°C (60–75°F).
Care Weak liquid feed monthly while actively growing.
Watering Provide enough to keep compost just moist. Do not overwater.

PHILODENDRON SCANDENS SWEETHEART VINE

A glossy-leaved climbing plant of the arum family, grown entirely for its shapely heart-like leaves (it produces no arum flowers in the home). Also known as the Heartleaf philodendron. In its native jungles it climbs trees, so looks its best when trained up a moss pole where its aerial roots can anchor.

Family Araceae.
Light Good light.
Temperature 13–24°C (55–75°F).
Care Liquid feed twice monthly.
Watering Moderate to avoid drying out. Mist leaves in summer to provide humidity.

PILEA CADIEREI ALUMINIUM PLANT

An attractive and very easily grown foliage plant, from South-Eastern Asia. It is also known as the aluminium plant from the raised silvery markings on its rich green leaves. It contrasts well with other foliage plants, especially perhaps coleus.

Family Urticaceae.
Light Dappled shade.
Temperature 18–24°C (65–75°F).
Care Liquid feed in spring and summer only, about twice a month.
Watering Moderate watering at all times and humid air.

PLUMBAGO AURICULATA CAPE LEADWORT

Still widely known as *P. capensis*, this plant is an untidy and scrambling South African shrub, treasured for its charming pale blue flowers. In the home it demands a light position and occasional pruning to keep it shapely, so is best planted in tub in a garden room.

Family Plumbaginaceae.
Light Full light and plenty of sun.
Temperature 15–24°C (60–75°F).
Care Liquid feed with high-potash twice monthly, when growing, to boost flowering.
Watering Plenty when growing to keep compost moist. Little in winter.

PRIMULA OBCONICA GERMAN PRIMROSE/POISON PRIMROSE

A Chinese species, this is one of several kinds grown as pot plants, and by far the most resilient. Its clusters of flowers may be rich magenta-red, pink, salmon, white or pale blue, and are long-lasting. It has a long flowering season, blooming from late winter to early summer.

Family Primulaceae.
Light Good light with some sun.
Temperature 10–15°C (50–60°F).
Care Liquid feed fortnightly while making flowers.
Watering Generous but do not waterlog.

PTERIS CRETICA CRETAN BRAKE/RIBBON FERN

A tender fern from Crete, it makes a neat bushy foliage pot plant and remains decorative. The form known as 'Albo-lineata', which has a creamy white band beside the midrib of each pinna, is more eyecatching and more suitable as a specimen plant.

Family Polypodiaceae.
Light Good light all year.
Temperature 15–24°C (60–75°F).
Care Weak liquid feed monthly while actively growing.
Watering Always keep moist. Plenty in summer, less in winter.

REBUTIA MINUSCULA CROWN CACTUS

Also known as the Mexican Sunball, these plants are rewarding because they are small and easy to accommodate on a sunny windowsill, and have attractive red flowers. They bloom early and increase quite rapidly forming offsets. The form Grandiflora has red flowers and those of Violaciflora are voilet.

Family Cactaceae.
Light Plenty of light.
Temperature 15–24°C (60–75°F).
Care Liquid feed every 3-5 weeks during growing season.
Watering Moderate when actively growing. Barely moist in winter.

RHIPSALIDOPSIS GAERTNERI EASTER CACTUS

Named after its flowering time, this is a jungle cactus that grows in the tropical rain forest of South America. The stems of this plant are formed of flat segments and its brick-red flowers are single or in small clusters at the tips of its stems. Blooms last a day or two but the display goes on for several weeks.

Family Cactaceae.
Light Moderate light.
Temperature 15–21°C (60–70°F).
Care High-potash feed twice a month in spring, none when at rest.
Watering Plenty until flowering is over. Little when resting.

RHOICISSUS RHOMBOIDEA GRAPE IVY/NATURAL VINE

A glossy-leaved creeper used for clothing trellis or for training over various kinds of support. The plant is correctly called *Cissus rhombifolia*, though its former name is more popular. The leaflets are formed of rhomboid shape; hence its name. It climbs on its own by means of tendrils.

Family Vitaceae.
Light Good light with some sun.
Temperature 15–24°C (60–75°F).
Care Liquid feed fortnightly when growing.
Watering Moderate when growing. Minimum in winter.

ROCHEA COCCINEA CRASSULA

A neat, rather rigid-growing succulent grown for its scarlet flowers, which open in midsummer, although nurseries force blooms in spring. An easily managed, colourful plant with six or more stems covered in triangular, leathery green leaves. The scented flowers are carried in clusters on top of these stems.

Family Crassulaceae.
Light Direct sun.
Temperature 15–24°C (60–75°F).
Care High-potash feed twice a month while flowering.
Watering Moderate in summer. Minimum in winter.

SAINTPAULIA IONANTHA AFRICAN VIOLET

This plant comes from Tanzania so it needs warmth and high humidity if the temperature is quite high. It hates draughts, so stand where it can be protected from air currents.

Family Gesneriaceae.
Light Good light, a west facing window is best in summer. Artificial light is needed to get flowers in winter.
Temperature 15–24°C (60–75°F).
Care Very weak liquid feed at each watering.
Watering Keep compost moist but let compost partly dry out between waterings. Keep water off leaves.

SANCHEZIA NOBILIS

A large plant grown for its handsome striped foliage. It does produce spikes of yellow flowers in autumn. The oval leaves, mid-green with yellow or off-white veins, cover this plant to soil level. A subtropical plant, it needs high humidity.

Family Acanthaceae.
Light Good light with some sun.
Temperature 15–24°C (60–75°F).
Care Liquid feed fortnightly when growing.
Watering Generous in summer, restrained in winter.

SANSEVIERIA TRIFASCIATA 'LAURENTII' SNAKESKIN PLANT

Commonly known as Mother-in-Law's Tongue, this plant is one of the toughest and least destructible house-plants. It withstands drought, rarely needs potting and always looks colourful. 'Laurentii' is a yellow-edged from of the species *S. trifasciata*, which has green leaves characterised by the snakeskin banding.

Family Agavaceae.
Light Bright light and plenty of sun.
Temperature 18–27°C (65–80°F).
Care Half-strength liquid feed once a month when growing only.
Watering Moderate when growing, minimum during winter.

SAXIFRAGA STOLONIFERA MOTHER OF THOUSANDS

A foliage plant grown for the colouring of its leaves and the plantlets which hang on long wiry stems. Tiny, starry white flowers are produced in late summer. Its habit makes it a suitable specimen for hanging baskets or on a shelf where the plantlets can hang freely.

Family Saxifragaceae.
Light Good light. 'Tricolour' needs more sun to maintain colouration.
Temperature 10–15°C (50–60°F).
Care Liquid feed monthly when growing.
Watering Plenty to keep moist while growing, little when at rest.

SCHLUMBERGERA BRIDGESII CHRISTMAS CACTUS

The much loved Christmas cactus is a jungle cactus, not a desert cactus. Flowering is triggered by short day-length and it does not always flower at Christmas, factors such as watering, warmth and hours of daylight will affect the timing.

Family Cactaceae.
Light Moderate in summer. Winter light suits it.
Temperature 15–24°C (60–75°F).
Care High potash liquid feed every two weeks from spring to autumn.
Watering Plentiful throughout the year except during short rest period.

SCINDAPSUS AUREUS DEVIL'S IVY/ POTHOS

More correctly known as *Epipremnum aureum,* this is a trailing plant from Polynesia. It is usually grown in a hanging basket, but can be trained up a moss pole. It evergreen leaves are splashed with gold; the variety 'Marble Queen' has white and green marbled leaves.

Family Araceae.
Light Bright light is essential.
Temperature 15–24°C (60–75°F).
Care Liquid feed fortnightly when growing.
Watering Moderate in summer; barely moist in winter.

SEDUM RUBROTINCTUM CHRISTMAS CHEER

Grown for its colourful foliage, green heavily tinted with red if kept warm and dry. The succulent leaves that form on its thin stems are plump and not unlike jelly beans. Taller stems tend to fall over and root into the compost. This sedum rarely flowers indoors.

Family Crassulaceae.
Light Good light in full sun.
Temperature 15–24°C (60–75°F).
Care No feeding necessary.
Watering Moderate while in growth, allow to partly dry out between waterings. Little in winter.

SETCREASEA PURPUREA PURPLE HEART

This is a fleshy-leaved trailing plant, closely related to the familiar trailing tradescantia, grown for its purple colouring. It needs a sunny spot to maintain its richest leaf colour, and a hanging pot or basket from which it can trail freely. It has tiny magenta-pink three-petalled flowers in mid-summer.

Family Commelinaceae.
Light Good light with some direct sun.
Temperature 18–24°C (65–75°F).
Care Liquid feed monthly when growing.
Watering Moderate but fairly dry between waterings.

SPATHIPHYLLUM WALLISII PEACE LILY

A glossy-leaved tropical evergreen grown for its foliage and white arum-like flowers, which develop in spring or summer. The spathes change from white to green after a week or so, but remain decorative for several weeks. A tolerant plant, it needs shade, warmth with humidity to replicate its jungle origins.

Family Araceae.
Light Moderate, never direct sun.
Temperature 15–24°C (60–75°F).
Care Weak liquid feed twice monthly while actively growing.
Watering Moderate when growing. Mist daily to deter red spider mite.

TRADESCANTIA FLUMINENSIS SPEEDY JENNY

The forms 'Variegata' and 'Quicksilver' (right) both have green and white striped leaves and are one of the most popular of all indoor hanging basket plants. They grow freely, are colourful and easily propagated. The leaves turn brown if the plant dries out and good light is needed to maintain the colour variegation.

Family Commelinaceae.
Light Good light and some sun.
Temperature 18–24°C (65–75°F).
Care Liquid feed twice a month while actively growing.
Watering Generous during active growth, restrained when semi-dormant.

VRIESIA SPLENDENS FLAMING SWORD

A tree-dwelling species, it forms the typical 'vase', which is a reservoir for moisture. When it is about five years old it produces a flower stem from the centre of its leaf rosette. This bears a brilliant red sword-shaped cluster of bracts from which short-lived, yellow flowers develop.

Family Bromeliaceae.
Light Good sunlight.
Temperature 15–24°C (60–75°F).
Care Weak liquid feed every two weeks from spring to autumn.
Watering Maintain a reservoir at the centre of the leaves, with soft water.

YUCCA ELEPHANTIPES SPINELESS YUCCA

These yuccas are not spiny but have soft foliage. As indoor plants they are often grown from Ti logs—lengths of woody stem which sprout to form sideshoots at the top. A foliage plant in a size convenient to accommodate in rooms. They never grow large enough to flower.

Family Agavaceae.
Light Good light and sunshine essential.
Temperature 15–24°C (60–75°F).
Care Liquid feed monthly while actively growing.
Watering Keep compost moist in summer. In winter water sparingly.

ZEBRINA PENDULA WANDERING JEW/SILVERY INCH PLANT

A fleshy-leaved trailing plant from Mexico and a relative of the tradescantia. It is well-named for its distinctly striped leaves have a green central stripe and green edges with silvery white areas. The form 'Purpusii' has purple-bronze leaves, and 'Quadricolour' has pink, cream, green and silver stripes.

Family Commelinaceae.
Light Good light and sun for colour.
Temperature 15–24°C (60–75°F).
Care Liquid feed fortnightly when growing.
Watering Moderate while growing, just moist in winter.

Index

Alphabetical listing of botanical names.

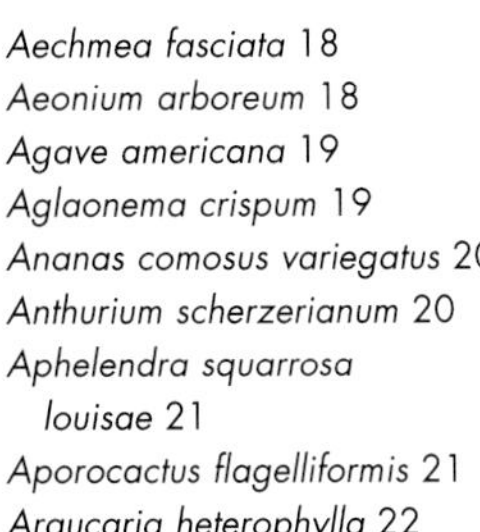

Index

Alphabetical listing of common names.